SHIREHAMPTON

1. The village green in about 1911. On the left is no.4, The Terrace c.1760's. From there to the gabled ended building to the right of the lamp are the grounds of "Walton House", the house behind the trees. In 1910-12 it was the home of Gilbert Jessop, cricketer, who played for the South of England against Australia in 1905, and often played for Shirehampton.

2. The Green c.1910 from the opposite direction. Park Hill leads up to the left, and across the corner is "Minto House", and Park Road runs right between it and "Keswick House" c.1760. "Minto House" was demolished in mid 1930s, and the Police Station was built on the foundations, today converted to flats.

3. Shirehampton Green in 1916, looking in the same direction as illustration no.1, with the coach house in middle distance of "Walton House". There are railings along the right hand side of the green. The Wellingtonia tree was planted to commemorate Queen Victoria's Jubilee.

4. Penpole Place c.1910. Left is "the Cottage" mentioned in March 1766, next is "Park House", and the first cottage beyond is No.9 Penpole Place, older villagers called it "Steepy Fields", leading to Penpole. The foreground area's old name is "The Batch".

SHIREHAMPTON

5. The High Street c.1905, "Walton House" on the left, then adjoining is Mr. M.L. Chubb, Postmaster and Stationer, and further along the large sign of Charlie Hodges Temperance Hotel. On the right is the old "George Inn". In 1903-1918 Harry Hobbs was the licensee.

6. Looking north down the High Street, with the Elizabethan House at the far end. The Wesleyan and Methodist church on the right was built in 1886. The second man on the right is thought to be Mr. A. A. Waite standing outside his ironmongers shop, which he opened in 1904.

7. This view of the High Street c.1909. Wilfred Bolwell opened his hairdressers, in 1908, on the left. Note the difference in Penpole Avenue side of the Wesleyan church. What is today the main entrance is here a little tower opening on to the High Street. The turret on top once housed a single bell.

8. A later view than No.7, looking towards the green. Mr Waite's ironmongers shop is on the left. The motor cycle and sidecar is outside J.S. Robsons who traded there only between 1924-27. The barbers pole of Wilf Bolwell is next to W.T. Meech leather goods, and by the sailor, C.H. Budd, outfitters and footwear. R.W. Parson's is licensee of the "Lifeboat".

9. Although "Walton House" is still off to the left and the fence and gate is visible. The coach house has been converted to a shop, the owners, Lennards, opened in 1928. The new "George Inn" was built on the site of the old "George" in 1929. Frank Adams Gainsford was licensee in 1935.

10. On the left is the "Lifeboat Inn", licenced for Georges Beers built around 1860. There have been changes to the frontage over the years, but it is still recognisable today. The stone pillars on the right are to Narford House which was demolished c.1930's. This picture c.1914.

11. St. Marys Church wall on the left, and beyond the large fir tree the railings of "Chapel House", the white house is Jack "pop" Wiltshires sweet shop, demolished for Coop store expansion. Opposite is the "Manor" or "Elizabethan House", built in the 16th century.

12. The ivy clad "Elizabethan" house c.1910, looking towards the centre of the village. On the right hand side by the entrance is the dairy. In 1927 its last occupier was George William Base. It was demolished for road-widening in late 1930s.

13. Station Road emerges in the centre of the village at the Green. This view c.1919, with the school on the left and beyond, behind the trees, are Winchester buildings c.1907. The four shops on the right are Nos. 1,2 and 3 Victoria Place, and on the corner of Pembroke Road, right, "Bristol House" known as Mrs Gard's to generations of children.

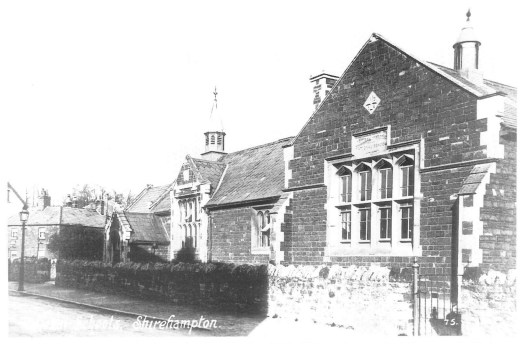

14. The National Schools in Station Road c.1900. This red stone building was built in 1849, with the right hand extension built in 1892. Previous headmaster James Wedmore was appointed in 1863, and lived in School Cottage, followed by James "Jasper" Banks in 1905. The school suffered bomb damage in 1939. School Cottage can be seen far left.

Station Road, Shirehampton.

15. Looking up Station Road towards the Green c.1933; beyond the villas on the left is the Roman Catholic church by Pembroke Avenue. The Savoy Cinema, not yet built, came in 1933. The pointed tower of the public hall, then the three semi detached houses were built 1923-25.

Shirehampton Parish Hall & Carnegie Library.

16. Shirehampton Public Hall and Carnegie Library in Station Road. The foundation stone was laid in 1903 by Mr. P. Napier-Miles. The library was one of 1,000 donated by Carnegie worldwide. Designed by Bligh Bond, who also designed Westward House and Wylands, it opened in 1905, the reading room having opened 1904.

17. St. Mary's Church c.1915, to the left is Pembroke Road and to the right the High Street. The single steel bell was first rung in December 1861, to commemorate the Prince Consorts funeral. It was destroyed by fire on Sunday 15th January 1928.

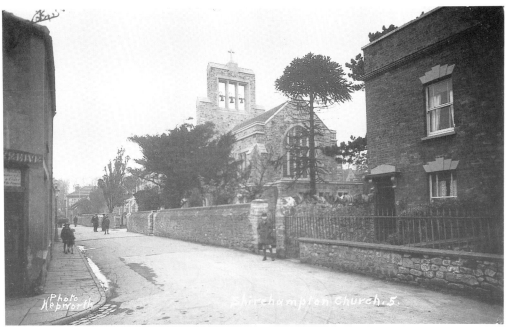

18. Looking at St. Mary's Church from the junction of Bradley Crescent, the "Beehive" and Pembroke Road. This new church was consecrated on 15th January 1930. The Centre bell was replaced by Electronic bells, a gift of the late Mrs Creber in 1959.

19. High Street in 1924. On the left, "Hermitage Cottages" and the "Hermitage". The partly demolished cottage above the boys was replaced along with "Chapel House" by the expansion of the co-op. The villas are 1, 2 and 3 "Shamrock Villas". Far right is "Westward House", the Miles estate office.

20. Bradley Crescent looking down from the junction with Pembroke Road. Maps of 1883 show about nineteen houses on the right hand side, with one small building on the left. At the time of this postcard, postally used in 1909, the shop no.2, is listed for 1905-09 as John Fuller, lamp and oil dealer.

21. Shirehampton Vicarage c.1910. The High Street is off right, also called The Priory. It was the vicarage from 1889 to 1951. The foundations of the Priory, originally built by the Monks of Cormeilles in Normandy.

22. The "Wylands", High Street called "Wylans" on maps of 1880, and was built on the site of a previous house, in c.1907. Early occupants were Captain and Mrs Scott, she was a matron of Kingsweston Hospital during the 1914-18 war. Mrs Kate Hill's nursing home in the early 1930s, it became a training school for G.P.O. engineering in 1935.

23. Looking down Lower High Street, with Old Barrow Hill the turning up left, and "Wylands Cottage" on the right. Straight down the hill are the gabled ends of "Bank Cottages". There was another cottage out of view to the right.

24. Lower Shirehampton. The stone wall on left is the footpath up to Old Quarry Road, and beyond the car, "Penpole House", used by the A.R.P. in the 1939-45 war was later demolished as it became unsafe.

25. Shirehampton Road c.1914, now named Lower High Street. By the cottage on the right is Penpole Lane. The horse drawn bakery van pulled by "Cricket" owned by Mary Ann Hack, whose shop was on the High Street, opposite the "Lifeboat Inn".

26. The same view as picture 25, in about 1941, trees and cottages are gone for a wider road, which was built in 1935-37. Semi detached houses, large street lamps and white lines in the middle of the road are familiar sights today.

27. Looking up Lower High Street towards the village, coming in on the left is Kingsweston Avenue by the large tree, and Meadow Grove going right opposite. This junction now has traffic lights, and many of the cottages by the man on the right survive today.

28. Looking from Kingsweston Avenue to Lower High Street, todays traffic light junction. Across the lower High Street is the gable of a cottage demolished to make way for Meadow Grove. While "Flowers Cottages" can be seen behind the trees, and are still there today. The houses in the foreground were some of the first council houses to be built in the village after the 1914-18 war.

29. After 1904, called Avonmouth Road, this is looking towards Shirehampton, with no.28 service gas-bag fitted bus coming towards Avonmouth c.1921. The man on the left is stood at the end of the lane to 'T' farm, and behind him and the hedge is "Shirehampton Farm". Road widening was approved in April 1911, to widen the road between Avonmouth Road and High Street from 36 feet to 60 feet.

30. Shirehampton Road, c.1917. The original track or road of this shown here may be one of those proposed in 1813 under the enclosures act. These roads would make the area of salt marsh more accessible. On Monday 12th April 1813, common rights to warths, moors, commons, wasterlands in the tything of Shirehampton ceased.

31. Shirehampton looking across from the Pill side of the ferry, the ferry boat moored by the slipway, on the far side. The white house is Wellington House, and next on the right the old "Lamplighters Inn", mentioned in Farleys Journal in 1767. The ferry closed in 1974.

32. P. & O. Campbells' paddle steamer "Westward Ho!" bound for the city docks seen from "Watch Tower Hill", Pill. Across the river the white building of the old river signal station, and further left Avonmouth Docks, c.1926-28.

33. The Portway towards the Avonmouth end, these double bay villas c.1927. The road off right is Grove Leaze, which leads right up into the village of Shirehampton.

34. The Portway where Station Road crosses from left to right, as yet no houses c.1926. The bus is no.99 service to Prince Street. The continuation of Station Road on the opposite side of the Portway leads to the Railway station, and "The Lamplighters Inn" near the Shirehampton-Pill ferry.

SHIREHAMPTON

35. Shirehampton Station opened originally in 1865 as a station on the Hotwells to Avonmouth line of the Bristol Port and Pier Railway, and after 1885 it was on the Clifton Extension railway via Montpelier and Clifton to Avonmouth. Closed to goods traffic in 1965, it remains open to passenger traffic on the Bristol Temple Meads to Severn Beach line.

36. The railway line near Shirehampton Station in 1907 looking towards the old iron bridge, near Horseshoe bend. The replacement bridge is built of concrete. The cottage on the left is "Laburnam Cottage", next door is "Rose Cottage", and over the bridge in the distance is "Fulligrove House" in Woodwell Road. The double track came into use in 1907, and the old Disc Signal on the right was removed later the same year.

37. Station Road c.1910, at the junction with Hung Road, and Springfield Avenue – the turning off on the left. The two large houses with boys outside the entrance are Nos. 1 and 2 Elm Villas. Mrs Creber, a music teacher, lived at No.1. The white house is Nos. 1 and 2 Alma Villas. The car HE 740 is parked outside "Overndale".

38. Further along Station Road towards the village green, the first shop on the left by the group of boys is Gilbert Howden, tailor and hairdresser c.1908. The villas centre distance are "Claire Villa", "Ingeldene" and "Belmont". On the right is School Cottage, and the National Schools. In 1933 the "Savoy" cinema opened where the iron railings are, right.

39. The Portway from Shirehampton Park c.1926, not long after its completion. No seats as yet is the viewing area, this view is looking towards Sea Mills. The double track of the railway line runs between Bristol Temple Meads and Avonmouth.

40. The Portway from the same vantage point looking in the opposite direction. The building on the left above the trees, the white house, is Myrtle Hall. The railway to Avonmouth crossed by Woodwell Bridge. In the distance on the right is Park Road.

41. The Horseshoe bend on the River Avon, a cargo ship being escorted up river by a tug. The white house on the Shirehampton side is the "Powder House", where ships deposited their gunpowder explosive before proceeding to the city docks. This practice dated from the late 18th century, the building is on B. Donn's map of 1769.

42. A three masted ship outward bound from the city docks c.1900. The flat area behind the ship on the Somerset side of the Avon was called "Sand Point" at one time. Over the years many ships came to grief on this bend of the river, known as Horseshoe Bend.

43. Looking up the Portway towards Sea Mills; c.1932-33 just beyond the lamp-post Woodwell Road comes up from the "Powder House", and continues to the village on the left. Portway School, now built beyond the houses on the left, opened in 1932. The houses were built in 1930.

44. An early view of the Portway taken not long after it was completed. It opened to traffic on 2nd of July 1926. A bus service commenced to run jointly with Bristol Tramways and the Greyhound Line. Park Road is the turning off right, Shirehampton village in the distance. Portway School opened on this corner with Park Road and the Portway in 1932.

45. The village green in Shirehampton c.1910, looking east, towards Park Hill. Park Road is a turning off right by "Keswick House". The stone wall left encircles "Sunny Hill" house. The fountain, centre, was built by Macfarlanes Saracen Foundry of Glasgow 1897.

46. Park Hill looking up to Shirehampton Lodge, at the top of the hill, and just beyond the golf links c.1910. The wall bottom right is to "Park Hill Farm". Just out of view on the left is "Sunny Hill Farm".

SHIREHAMPTON

47. Looking down Park Hill, with "Park Lodge" on the left – old maps give it as "Shirehampton Lodge". This view c.1911. The toll gates to Squire Miles' Kingsweston estate were removed c.1915. Beyond the gates by the lamp post is the entrance to "Oldfield House". "Sunny Hill Farm" is down the hill in the centre.

48. As picture 47 in summer c.1914. Miss Helen Jefferies lived with her family at 'The Lodge' from 1910 to 1921/22 and she remembers closing the gates when remount horses got away from the "dips" on Penpole in the 1914 war. She also remembers soldiers lifting equipment over these toll gates en route for the battle of Mons. The gates were removed during the war.

49. Penpole Lane looking towards Shirehampton Park to where the 1914 War Memorial came in 1921, with "Wood Lodge" on the left. The toll gate is swung open, c.1908.

50. "Wood Lodge" the toll keepers cottage at the Penpole entrance to Shirehampton Park. This view c.1913, with Shirehampton Cricket ground situated beyond the fence on the right.

51. Shirehampton War memorial to commemorate the 58 local men who gave their lives in the 1914-18 war, built on land donated by Mr. P. Napier-Miles, at the corner with Penpole Lane and Shirehampton Road. It was dedicated by the Archdeacon of Bristol on September 4th 1921, and unveiled by General C.E. Bruce C.M.G., D.S.O.

52. Penpole Lane looking towards Avonmouth, Penpole Point up to the right, c.1915. A delightful rural view, note the caption says near Bristol. Portway Upper School is now to the left of the lane.

53. "Penpole Lodge", Penpole Point, also known in the old days as "Belvedere", also the "Breakfast room". This was the lodge to Kings Weston Estate, Open air services were held near there annually led by St. Mary's Church Choir at Rogationtide. It was demolished c.1952.

54. In front of the lodge is the "sundial", with its circular seat, and children posing for the camera in c.1920's. The sundial has a varied history, as to its origin. In 1688 the Merchant Ventures voted £5 for repairs to the "Compass" on Penpole Hill.

View from Penpole Point, Shirehampton.

55. The tall chimney and the cluster of houses above the word "view" is West Town, bombed 16/17 January 1941, so badly damaged that the houses were never rebuilt. The oil tanks to the left of the "sundial" are Anglo-American oil at Broadpill. To the far right John Robinson's old Granary building.

View from Penpole Point, Shirehampton.

56. From the bottom of Penpole bank, Old Quarry Road and Kingsweston Avenue. In the centre distance can be seen a Fair with its helter-skelter, and other side shows. This is on the Avonmouth side of West Town lane c.1930s. The wooden fence protects the drop into the old quarry.

57. Shirehampton Road when still a narrow road within Kingsweston Park, c.1911. On the left is "The Rush Pool", and "Kingsweston House" is in the centre distance, home of Mr. P. Napier-Mills, between 1881 when his father died till his death in 1935. The golf course is on the right.

Rush Pool, Shirehampton Park.

58. The same view in the early 1930s. The "Rush Pool" is partly filled in by the fence, and the road widened and made a public road since the first World War. A bus is on its way to the Tramway Centre, the 1914 War Memorial is to its left.

59. The east side of "Kingsweston House" when it was an Auxiliary Forces Hospital from 1915-19. Mrs Miles, wife of the estate owner, was a matron and for a time Mrs Walter Scott who lived at "Wylands" served as nursing matron there.

60. "Kingsweston House" taken in the same period during the First World War. Soldiers recovering from their injuries wander on the drive. The balustrades re-erected here in 1873, came from Bristol Bridge, removed from there during extensive alterations to the bridge.

61. "Kingsweston Inn", an old coaching inn standing on "Abbots Way", an old track from Blaize Castle across the downs to Shirehampton. It was built in the late 17th century by Sir Robert Southwell, his coat of arms are carved over the door. It later became part of the Miles estate.

62. "Kingsweston Inn" some ten years later in 1915. The notice over the door advertises "Teas and Accommodation". No doubt the festive crowd are enjoying refreshments, sitting at long tables and tressel seats. The large tree on the left is known as "the old man".

63. The iron bridge c.1905, looking towards Henbury. It connected Shirehampton Park with Kingsweston Down when Kings Weston Road was carved out of the hill, replacing the narrow track in front of "Kingsweston Inn".

64. "Kingsweston Cottages" adjoining "Kingsweston Inn", the tree on the right is the "old man", *(see illustration no. 62)*. The cottages from left to right are nos. 4, 5 and 6. The track in front is part of the old original road.

THE HOUSE IN THE GARDENS, SHIREHAMPTON.   41804

65. The "House in the Garden" built in 1937 for the widow of the squire, Mr. P. Napier-Miles, after the Kingsweston Estate was sold in 1936 to pay death duties relating to the late squire. This view is before 1954 as Bewy's Cross was re-erected in that year.

THE FISH POND KINGSWESTON BRISTOL.   32073.

66. The fish pond adjoining the "House in the Garden", in Napier Mills Road, situated opposite the stables of Kingsweston House. Mrs Miles died in June 1948, and the "House in the Garden" was bought by Bristol Corporation and used as a school for sub-normal girls. This card was postally used in October 1948.

67. Sea Mills station opened originally on the Hotwells to Avonmouth line of the Bristol Post and Pier Railway, and after 1885 ran via Montpelier and Clifton to Avonmouth. It currently operates passenger services on the Bristol T.M. to Severn Beach. It has never handled goods traffic.

68. The railway bridge after leaving Sea Mills station. In the foreground are the remains of the docks built by Joshua Franklin in 1712, on the site of the original Roman dock which was used until 1766, when it fell into disrepair. Light pleasure boats can be seen moored on this postcard which was posted in 1935.

69. The viaduct bridge carrying the Portway, completed in 1926, connects Hotwells with Avonmouth, is five miles in length and cost £800,000. The water flowing under the central span is the River Trym, which flows into the River Avon at this point. Through the right arch can be seen the tress bordering Sea Mills Lane.

70. Looking in roughly the same direction as illustration 69, before the Portway was built. The lady artist with her easel is standing by ruined walls by the old Roman Harbour. To the right is the track before Sea Mills Lane was built. This picture is from about 1910.

Kingsweston Down, showing Sea Mills, Bristol.

71. A view of Sea Mills from Kingsweston Down. The council houses are the estate first built under the Addison plan of 1919. The first houses, built in the early 1920's, filling a great need for affordable housing after the First World War.

General View, Sea Mills Park.

72. The estate was first called Sea Mills Park, and houses continued to be built through the 1920's. This view is Shirehampton Road, where Sylvan Way, near the first bus, crosses from left to right. The bus further on is parked in Sea Mills Square.

Shirehampton Rd, Sea Mills Park.

354
PHOTO
HEPWORTH.

73. Shirehampton Road looking in the opposite direction to illustration 72. The single decker bus is enroute for Shirehampton and Avonmouth. This card was postally used in 1928.

Shirehampton Road. Sea Mills Park

200
PHOTO
HEPWORTH

74. Further up Shirehampton Road towards Kingsweston Down, the trees in the background are on the Down. This view c.1929, the turning by the girls is High Grove, with houses still being built behind, in Elberton Road.

75. A winter view of the council houses, one of several roads ending with Leaze, built to the right of Sea Mills Square, coming from Shirehampton. This card was postally used in 1928.

76. Riverleaze, built in the same style as illustration 75, but with shutters only to the downstairs windows, c.1928.

77. The Pentagon with a street lamp in the centre of the grass area, is a junction which connects several roads. St. Edyths Road leads to Sea Mills Square, with Woodleaze off to the left. This card was postally used in 1928.

78. Sylvan Way, showing another example of a grass junction with a street lamp. This road is one of the longest in Sea Mills running from the Portway to Dingle Road in Coombe Dingle. This card was postally used in 1935.

79. Brookleaze, with neat hedges, and trees growing in the grass verges. It extends from The Pentagon crossing Failand Walk and Crescent, and connects with Meadway and Trymleaze.

80. Woodleaze, children well dressed standing for the photographer in this winter view c.1924. It connects with Sylvan Way and The Pentagon. Bay windows are a feature of some of these houses.

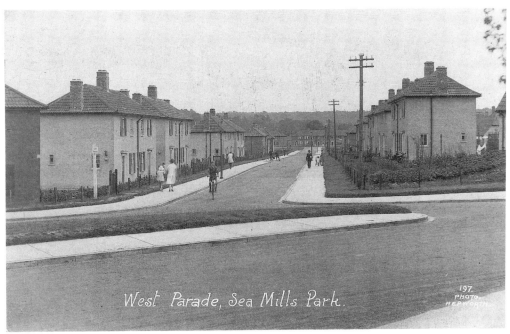

81. West Parade on the left hand side of Sea Mills Square coming from Shirehampton. It joins the Square to the left of Sea Mills Methodist Church, crossing The Crescent.

82. East Parade joins the Square on the right hand side of the Methodist Church, also crossing The Crescent. The houses on the left are built of red brick, and on the opposite corner of the pavement is a water hydrant.

83. An aerial view of the Recreation ground c.1930's, showing the extensive area of Sea Mills towards Kingsweston Down. The roads either side are Riverleaze and St. Edyths Road.

84. Sea Mills Square c.1938, with Sea Mills Methodist Church on the far side, a single decker bus is parked, passengers just having alighted. Although Sea Mills was developed with houses from the early 1920's the shops, built on four corners of the square, weren't built until 1929.

85. Trym Side, a road built adjoining the "Leaze" roads, between the Portway and Shirehampton Road. This road joins with Riverleaze, and Meadway, c.1930.

86. Looking from Stoke Bishop towards Sea Mills. The trees centre distance are in Trym Side Park, near the junction with Sea Mills Lane on the left, and opposite "The Mill House Inn", on the corner of Shirehampton Road and Bell Barn Lane, c.1930's.

INDEX

SHIREHAMPTON

SEA MILLS